DRACULA RIDES AGAIN

A Halloween Western

Jeff Goode

BROADWAY PLAY PUBLISHING INC
224 E 62nd St, NY, NY 10065
www.broadwayplaypub.com
info@broadwayplaypub.com

DRACULA RIDES AGAIN
© Copyright 2006 by Jeff Goode

All rights reserved. This work is fully protected under the copyright laws of the United States of America. No part of this publication may be photocopied, reproduced, stored in a retrieval system, or transmitted, in any form or by any means, electronic, mechanical, recording, or otherwise, without the prior permission of the publisher. Additional copies of this play are available from the publisher.

Written permission is required for live performance of any sort. This includes readings, cuttings, scenes, and excerpts. For amateur and stock performances, please contact Broadway Play Publishing Inc. For all other rights please contact the author at jeffgoode.com.

First printing: January 2006
I S B N: 0-88145-277-7

Book design: Marie Donovan
Word processing: Microsoft Word
Typographic controls: Xerox Ventura Publisher 2.0 P E
Typeface: Palatino
Printed and bound in the U S A

DRACULA RIDES AGAIN opened on 19 October 1995 at the Theater of the American West in Republican City, Nebraska. The cast and creative contributors were:

OLD TIMER .... Julie Haussermann
THE COUNT .... Charles Davies
JESSE CLANTON .... Beau Hamilton
JAKE CLANTON .... Lucy Duda
DELLA .... Kris Davies
MARIETTA .... Lucy Duda
TOWNSPERSON 1 .... Susan Potter
TOWNSPERSON 2 .... Lucy Duda
TOWNSPERSON 3 .... Beau Hamilton
TOWNSPERSON 4 .... Julie Haussermann
MAYOR .... Mel Keller
BUTCH CLANTON .... Susan Potter
DOC FRANKENSTEIN .... Lisa Harrison

Direction, scenery & lighting .... Charles Davies
Costume design .... Kris Davies

CHARACTERS

THE COUNT
DELLA
DOC
SHERIFF
OLD TIMER
BARKEEP
MARIETTA
MAYOR
MILLIE MAE
FRANKENSTEIN MONSTER

THE CLANTONS:
JUDD, JODY, JESSE, JAMIE, JOSIE, JETHRO, JANGO & BUTCH

TOWNSPEOPLE, CARD PLAYERS, PIANO PLAYER, SHOWGIRLS, *etc.*

THE MUMMY

PRODUCTION NOTES

Scene design: DRACULA RIDES AGAIN was originally conceived as a series of featured scenes played on a wild west saloon set—which would occupy most of the stage—alternating with shorter scenes on smaller, "suggested" sets, taking place downstage of the main set, or in front of the curtain, or possibly off to one side in a dedicated "swing" set area.

This is not necessarily how you will want to stage the production yourself, but being aware of this convention may help you follow the alternation of locations in the play.

The Mummy stagehand: During rehearsals for the original production, director Charles Davies pointed out that the only archetypal movie monster missing from the play was the Mummy. A Mummy Stagehand was added as a way of including that character in the show without altering the existing plotline. (And because it would be funny to see blind-folded stagehands crashing into things.)

This part of the play is completely optional. You should feel free to omit the Mummy, if you like. (Or feel free to dress *all* your stagehands as blind mummies. That would be funny, too.)

Gender roles: The playwright encourages color-blind and gender-blind casting—choosing the best person for the part, regardless of their own race or gender. It is not necessary, for example, for Doc Frankenstein to be played by someone of German descent.

You should also feel free to *change* the gender of any of the characters to fit your pool of actors. The effect of some changes may vary, of course—forcing the Mayor to dress as a showgirl, for example, will have different connotations if the character is male rather than female—but in general, there is nothing gender-specific about the overall theme of the play, so there's no reason not to adjust the cast of characters to suit your own company.

The Clantons: The Clanton boys...or girls...or both...are a posse of hench-deputies for the villains of the show. Although some of them have been given individual character names in the script, they mainly serve, as a group, to wreak mayhem and to allow the play to have a ridiculously high body count. As such, their roles may be combined or redistributed, as necessary, to create a posse of whatever size or composition your production desires.

Note: If you choose to have an all-girl or all-boy clan of Clantons, be sure to omit the running gag about "the Clanton boys...and girls."

my thanks to
Charles Davies
and the
Theater of the American West
without whom, this play simply would not exist

ACT ONE

OLD TIMER: *(Singin':)* I remember the evenin'
He rode into town.
The moon it was full
And there wasn't a sound
'Cept the coyotes howlin' that filled up the night.
Said, "They call me the Count. I'm just in for a bite."

THE SALOON

(Nighttime. Merry saloon music plays in a minor key. Howling off in the distance. The COUNT *walks into the saloon. Long black cape, spurs jangling. Abruptly, the music stops and the piano player darts out of sight. The* COUNT *goes to the bar, where the surly* BARKEEP *cleans her dirty glasses with a dusty rag.)*

BARKEEP: What'll it be, stranger?

COUNT: Bloody Mary.

(The BARKEEP *lunges across the bar, grabs the* COUNT *by the collar and thrusts a six-gun in his face.)*

BARKEEP: What'd you call me?

(The COUNT *calmly crushes the* BARKEEP's *hand.)*

COUNT: Never mind. I'll get it myself.

(The COUNT *drops the* BARKEEP *and goes behind the bar, starts mixing himself a Bloody Mary. Two nasty-looking galoots,* JUDD *and* JODY CLANTON *saunter up to the bar.)*

JUDD: What the heck is that concoction?

JODY: Looks like a glass o' blood.

COUNT: It's a mixed drink made with tomato juice and—

JUDD: *(Viciously:)* DID I ASK YOU?

COUNT: No. I suppose not. Sorry to interrupt.

JODY: We don't like strangers 'round these parts.

COUNT: Then perhaps I should introduce myself—

JUDD: WE DON'T LIKE STRANGERS EVEN ONCE WE GETS TO KNOW 'EM!

COUNT: Well, then. *(Toasting:)* Salud.

(He drinks. The CLANTONS *snicker.)*

JODY: Looks like he's drinkin' a glass o' blood, Judd.

JUDD: I reckon that makes him a blood sucker, don't it?

JODY: Are you a blood sucker, stranger?

COUNT: Are you trying to get to know me?

*(*JUDD *and* JODY *angrily draw their pistols, point them at the* COUNT's *head.)*

COUNT: I don't suppose those are silver bullets?

JUDD: You talk too much, stranger.

JODY: He sure does, Judd, he talks too much.

JUDD: We don't like people what's all talk.

JODY: No sir, that's not the kind o' people we take kindly to.

COUNT: Me neither.

(In a deft display, the COUNT *suddenly yanks* JUDD *over the bar, grabs* JODY *by the gun hand, twists it away from her face and bites her on the wrist.* JODY *drops her gun and runs out*

ACT ONE

of the saloon. The COUNT *turns to* JUDD, *lying on the floor behind the bar. His cape billows, bat-like, as he swoops down upon the helpless man. Suddenly,* DELLA, *a showgirl, appears at the top of the stairs. The* COUNT, *sensing her entrance, stops what he's doing and looks up.)*

DELLA: Howdy, stranger. Welcome to Tombstone.

COUNT: I don't think I like being a stranger in this town.

*(*DELLA *makes a long, sultry cross down the stairs, across the room and over to him at the bar.)*

DELLA: Then why'd you come back?

COUNT: Who says I'm back?

DELLA: You look awful back.

COUNT: You act awful forward.

(She slaps him.)

COUNT: All right, if you must know, I came back because I heard the prettiest dance hall girl in all of three states might be in some kind of trouble.

DELLA: Is this one of those states?

COUNT: If you're here, it might as well be all fifty.

DELLA: Thirty-eight.

COUNT: That's right. Thirty-eight.

DELLA: That's sweet of you to say.

COUNT: It's just a number.

DELLA: And you're just a Count.

COUNT: So *are* you in trouble?

DELLA: Not just me. The whole town's in trouble, Count. Since you left there ain't been nothin' but trouble.

COUNT: And you want me to help?

DELLA: Isn't that what I said in my letter?

COUNT: I don't know what you said in your letter. It came to me Pony Express. The rider was attacked by renegades, and this is all I got.

(He hands her a tiny fragment of paper.)

DELLA: "Dear Count..."

(He hands her another fragment.)

DELLA: "Love, Della."

(Their eyes meet.)

COUNT: Did you mean it when you said, "Love, Della"?

DELLA: Did you mean it when you said you'd come back for me one day?

(He hangs his head in shame. She takes that as a "no" and slaps him again.)

COUNT: I would have come back for you, Della, but I knew you could never love me.

DELLA: I would have loved you, but I knew you would never come back.

COUNT: I would have come back.... No, we did that already.

DELLA: That's all behind us now, Count. This town needs you.

COUNT: This town needs me like it needs another hole in its head.

DELLA: Compared to the great big one we dug ouselves into, a little head hole don't sound so bad. There's a new Sheriff in Tombstone.

COUNT: Nothing you can't handle.

DELLA: A she-Sheriff.

COUNT: Oh.

ACT ONE

DELLA: And she's a ruthless, lowdown snake-in-the-grass.

COUNT: At least she's not yellow-bellied and good-for-nothing.

DELLA: No, but the thing she's good for is taking over the whole town and running it into the ground. Her and her gang of so-called deputies. The Clanton brothers. And sisters.

COUNT: The Clantons, huh?

DELLA: That's two of 'em you met just now. Judd and Jody Clanton. But there's plenty more where they came from.

COUNT: They don't seem so tough.

DELLA: Maybe not to you, Count. But ordinary folks is terrified of 'em. They've got us all so spooked, we're afraid of our own shadows. *(Seeing her shadow:)* AAGH! *(She recovers:)* Make no mistake, the Clantons are the meanest orneriest bunch o' sidewinders this side o' the other side o' town.

COUNT: And what's on the other side of town?

DELLA: The Sheriff. And her silent partner. The one they call...Doc.

COUNT: *(Suspicious:)* A doctor? And he's silent?

DELLA: As a grave.

COUNT: That's my kind o' silent.

DELLA: If somebody doesn't stop the two of them soon, they're gonna turn Tombstone into a ghost town.

COUNT: And that's bad?

DELLA: *(Throwing herself in his arms:)* I'm awful scared, Count.

COUNT: You've never been one to let a little ruckus rattle you, Della. Weren't you the one who told me, "If you can't take the heat, go to Boston"?

DELLA: "If you can't take the heat, go to heck" is what I said.

COUNT: Just trying to be polite.

DELLA: There's no ladies present, Count, and you know it.

COUNT: So what's troubling you, Della? The new Sheriff?

DELLA: No, it's the other one. The Doc.

COUNT: What about him?

DELLA: He *wants* me, Count. He wants me in a way no man has ever wanted me before.

COUNT: I didn't know there were any more ways to want you.

DELLA: He wants me...experimentally.

COUNT: Yeah, that's a new one.

DELLA: You gotta help me, Count. And if not me, do it for us. And if not us, do it for me in a different outfit.

COUNT: The little black number with the veil and petticoat?

DELLA: It's right upstairs.

COUNT: Okay, I'll do it.

(MARIETTA *leaps onstage.*)

MARIETTA: Yahoo!

(MARIETTA *is another showgirl, who has apparently been eavesdropping on their conversation the whole time.*)

DELLA: You hear that, Marietta? He's gonna do it!

ACT ONE 7

MARIETTA: Can I watch?

DELLA: First, go wake the Mayor and tell him the good news!

COUNT: And then wake the whole town and tell them to meet here at the saloon right away.

(MARIETTA *rushes out.*)

DELLA: What do you want the whole town for?

COUNT: I can't do this alone, Della. While I'm gone, I want you to organize the townspeople into political action groups.

DELLA: Where are you going?

COUNT: To the other side of town. I'm gonna pay the Sheriff a little visit.

DELLA: I don't know how to thank you, Count.

(*They gaze into each other's eyes.*)

COUNT: Well...

DELLA: No, you're right, I do know how to thank you.

(*Sounds of an angry posse approaching*)

COUNT: What's that?

DELLA: It's the Clantons!

(*The* COUNT *draws his pistol.*)

DELLA: No, no, you'd better go. If they find you here—

(JODY *bursts in.*)

JODY: I found him!

(*Enter* JESSE *and* BUTCH, *as well. They surround the* COUNT.)

BUTCH: This the fella that bit you, Jody?

JODY: Yep, that's him, all right.

(BUTCH *turns to the* COUNT.)

BUTCH: So you must be the one they call... "The guy that bit me".

COUNT: And you must be the one they call... (*Looks her up and down:*) "Butch".

(JODY *and* JESSE *gasp.*)

BUTCH (*Livid:*) I don't know how you knew that, stranger, but I'll thank you to call me Deputy!

COUNT: You're welcome...Deputy. Now, I want to speak to your boss. The Sheriff.

BUTCH: I know who my boss is! And you'll speak to the Sheriff when I'm darn good 'n ready to let you speak to the Sheriff, and not a minute before. Or after. And in the meantime... (*Cracks knuckles*) I think you and me's gonna have a little "chat". And then I think Jesse might want a word with you. And after that, Jody's got a little something she'd like to discuss. And then, Jake and Jack'll be along to confer with you on a related subject, and then—

COUNT: (*Interrupting:*) I'm not one for polite conversation—if I understand your metaphor—but unless you all back away real slow... You're gonna have a symposium on your hands.

(*The* COUNT's *fingers twitch on the handle of his revolver. The* CLANTONS *all strike gun-fighting stances, hands hover near their holsters.*)

BUTCH: Please, stranger, speak freely! My colleagues and I are eager to engage you in the kind of spirited debate which this great nation was founded upon.

(*The* COUNT *eyes the three adversaries squared off against him. Tense pause. The* COUNT *makes a move for his gun and all three of them beat him to the draw. He is shot several times. When the smoke clears, the* COUNT *is still standing.*)

ACT ONE

Slowly, he draws his gun from its holster... Then he drops dead. Piano music resumes, and the CLANTONS *hoot and cheer.)*

(Blackout)

(The MUMMY *stagehand crosses the stage, arms outstretched, like a mummy—or like someone who can't see because they have bandages over their eyes— moaning mummy-like, and exits. It comes back in with the Sheriff's Office set, places it. It starts off again, but can't see for the bandages, crashes into a wall, feels around for the door, then exits.)*

THE SHERIFF'S OFFICE

(The SHERIFF, *an Annie Oakley-type, is getting the latest news from the* CLANTONS.*)*

SHERIFF: And then you shot him?

JESSE: Yep.

SHERIFF: Dead?

JESSE: Yep.

SHERIFF: And that's the whole the story?

JESSE: Yep.

SHERIFF: I hate that story! That's a stupid story. Don't ever tell me a stupid story like that again. When I ask you for news, I want news. I don't want to hear about every time you yahoos kick a dog!

JESSE: *(Cowed:)* Yes, Sheriff.

SHERIFF: Is there anything else?

JESSE: *(Hesitant:)* Well...

SHERIFF: What?!

JESSE: We kicked a dog.

SHERIFF: Get out of here!

(JESSE *exits. Suddenly, the* SHERIFF *senses a figure silhouetted in the doorway. She spins around, quick as lightning, and draws her gun. Enter* DOC FRANKENSTEIN.)

SHERIFF: Doc!

DOC: Morning, Sheriff.

SHERIFF: I almost shot your fool head off.

DOC: Are you calling me a fool, Sheriff?

SHERIFF: No, Doc, of course not. It's just you shouldn't sneak up on me like that. You know I got a hair-trigger trigger finger.

DOC: I hear there was some trouble at the saloon.

SHERIFF: Nothin' my deputies can't handle.

DOC: I hope not. For your sake.

SHERIFF: Are you threatening me, Doc?

DOC: Yes, I think I am. I don't need trouble. Not now. When my work is so near its completion. And if you can't keep the peace in this town... Well, I think you know what I mean when I say... You can be "replaced".

SHERIFF: *(Unnerved:)* I sure do.

DOC: Good.

(DOC *starts to leave, then he spins around and draws his pistol, quicker than lightning. He is faster than the* SHERIFF. *He blows imaginary smoke off the barrel of his gun as he smiles and walks out.)*

(Blackout)

(The MUMMY *enters. It picks up the* SHERIFF's *set and tries to exit. It gets through the door on the third try.)*

ACT ONE   11

THE SALOON

(DELLA *stares forlornly out a window.* MARIETTA *rushes in with the* MAYOR.)

MARIETTA: Della, I got the Mayor!

DELLA: You're too late.

MAYOR: I came as quick as I could!

DELLA: It's nine o'clock in the morning! I sent for you last night.

MAYOR: You woke me out of bed, Della. I had to get dressed.

DELLA: It took you nine hours to dress yourself?

MARIETTA: Now, Della, it's not all the Mayor's fault.

MAYOR: That's right. While I was pullin' on my drawers, Marietta and I got to talkin' about the sad state of affairs in Tombstone, and how it's not safe to walk the streets at night anymore, what with the Clantons on the loose and all. And we got to wonderin' how we were going to get back to the saloon safely, it bein' night and all, and it not being safe to walk the streets at night.

MARIETTA: And then we got to talkin' about how somebody ought to do something about that. How there oughta be a law or something.

MAYOR: And then we got to talkin' about laws and lawmaking, and how a bill becomes a law.

MARIETTA: And then the Mayor said the funniest thing, about how politics is strange bedfellows.

MAYOR: And then Marietta said something even funnier about how there's three things you're not supposed to discuss at the supper table:

MAYOR & MARIETTA: *(In unison:)* Politics, religion and sex.

(They both laugh.)

MAYOR: And I pointed out that we wasn't at the supper table.

MARIETTA: So, of course we got to talkin' about religion.

MAYOR: And one thing led to another and to make a long story short—

MARIETTA: We covered all three of them topics.

MAYOR: That's right.

DELLA: For nine hours???

MARIETTA: Yep. Fifteen minutes for politics, ten minutes for religion—

MAYOR: I came as quick as I could.

DELLA: Well, you shoulda came sooner! *(She storms out.)*

MARIETTA: Della, wait, where are you going?

(Just then, some other TOWNSPEOPLE *rush in, also still getting dressed.)*

TOWNSPEOPLE: We came as quick as we could!

MAYOR: Well, you can all go home. Della's in a snit.

MILLIE MAE: But why'd she wake us all out of bed? She knows it's not safe to walk the streets at night. What was so danged important?

MAYOR: I don't know.

MILLIE MAE: Well, who knows?

MAYOR: Nobody knows.

ACT ONE 13

MARIETTA: I know.

MAYOR: You do?

MARIETTA: Sure. Didn't I tell you?

MAYOR: No, what is it, Marietta? Is it bad news?

MARIETTA: No, it's the best kind of news.

TOWNSPEOPLE: What? What? What??

MARIETTA: He's come back!

MAYOR: He's back?

MARIETTA: He rode into town last night.

TOWNSPEOPLE: Yahoo!

MARIETTA: He was right here in the saloon. Sittin' right there on that barstool.

(Several TOWNSPEOPLE *squeal and grab the barstool, fighting over it and breaking it into many pieces.)*

MAYOR: This is the greatest day in the history of Tombstone!

MARIETTA: Our troubles are over.

MILLIE MAE: What do we do now, Mayor?

MAYOR: Get out the bullwhips and piñatas. We're gonna have us a party!

TOWNSPEOPLE: Yahoo!

MAYOR: *(To* MARIETTA*:)* Now, you're sure it was him?

MARIETTA: Sure as I'm sittin' here.

(Realizing she's not sitting, MARIETTA *quickly pulls up a chair.)*

MAYOR: Did you talk to him? Did it sound like him?

MARIETTA: Mostly he talked to Miss Della, but it was definitely him. I'd recognize him anywhere.

(TOWNSPEOPLE *squeal.*)

MILLIE MAE: Was he tall and handsome?

MARIETTA: Just like you'd imagine.

MILLIE MAE: With his hair slicked back, and a big cape like in the movies?

MARIETTA: Yep.

MILLIE MAE: A big white cape trimmed with rhinestones and sequins?

MARIETTA: Uh, no, a black cape.

MILLIE MAE: Black?

MAYOR: What was he doing in a black cape?

MARIETTA: He always wears a black cape.

MILLIE MAE: He never wore a black cape before.

MAYOR: You must be confused.

MARIETTA: Well, I am now.

MAYOR: Are we talkin' about the same fella?

MARIETTA: Who do you think we're talkin' about?

MAYOR & TOWNSPEOPLE: Elvis!

(*Beat*)

MARIETTA: I may have misled you.

(*The* TOWNSPEOPLE *groan and give back the pieces of the barstool.*)

MAYOR: Well, then who are you talkin' about, Marietta?

MARIETTA: Miss Della's gunfighter friend.

MAYOR: A gunfighter? Here in Tombstone?

MARIETTA: Miss Della sent for him to help us.

MILLIE MAE: Is he fast?

ACT ONE 15

MAYOR: Is he mean?

MILLIE MAE: Is he gonna get rid of the Clantons?

MARIETTA: I think that's the general idea.

TOWNSPEOPLE: Who is he? Have we heard of him?

MARIETTA: He called himself...The Count.

TOWNSPEOPLE: The Count!!!

(The TOWNSPEOPLE *scream and run around in a panic.)*

MAYOR: *(Terrified:)* What's the Count doing here?

MARIETTA: I told you, Miss Della sent for him. He's gonna help us. He's gonna take on the Sheriff and her boys. And girls.

TOWNSPEOPLE: Yahoo!!

MAYOR: The Count's come to save us! This is the greatest thing to happen in this town since—since Elvis almost came.

TOWNSPEOPLE: Yahoo!!

*(*PIANO PLAYER *starts playing as people celebrate. Gunfire offstage.* PIANO PLAYER *stops.)*

MILLIE MAE: *(Looking out a window:)* It's the Clantons! And they're headed this way!

(People run around screaming and run off, leaving only the MAYOR *and* MARIETTA.*)*

MAYOR: The Clantons! What are we gonna do? They're gonna think we're up to something!

MARIETTA: We *are* up to something.

MAYOR: Yeah, but they don't need to know that.

MARIETTA: Don't let 'em scare you, Mayor. We got the Count on our side, now. Compared to him, the Clantons ain't nothin' but a bunch of hooligans in stylish bandanas.

(The CLANTONS—JESSE, JAMIE *and* BUTCH—*saunter into the saloon, surround the* MAYOR *and* MARIETTA.*)*

JESSE: *(Intimidatingly:)* Well, well, well, if it ain't the early bird and her worm.

(MARIETTA *nudges the nervous* MAYOR. *He musters all his swagger.)*

MAYOR: And if it ain't the Clanton brothers. And sisters. Jesse and Jamie and Butch.

BUTCH: Don't call me Butch!

MAYOR: *(Flinching:)* Sorry bout that, Winnie June. *(Regaining his bluster:)* So, what brings you here at this hour?

JESSE: We could ask you the same question, Mayor.

MAYOR: Well then, ask away, Jesse!

JESSE: What brings you here at this hour, Mayor?

MAYOR: The horse I rode in on!

(MARIETTA *and the* MAYOR *burst out laughing at his joke, bewildering the* CLANTONS.*)*

JESSE: That ain't funny.

MARIETTA: No, but your face is *killing* me!

(MARIETTA *and the* MAYOR *laugh some more.)*

JESSE: My face won't be the only thing killing you, if you don't knock it off.

MAYOR: Oh yeah? Well, pardon my French, but I don't think you've got the cojones!

JESSE: And I think you forget who you're talkin' to ...Lester.

THE OTHER CLANTONS: Ooooh.

ACT ONE

MAYOR: As I recall, I'm talkin' to the rootin'est... Tootin'est... Tootie-frootin'est bunch of polecats that ever sweet-talked a bow-legged mare.

JESSE: Why, them's fightin' words, Mayor!!

MAYOR: Then I guess you better start fightin'!

(JESSE *and* JAMIE *start fighting with each other.* JAMIE *gets thrown through a window.*)

MAYOR: And as for you, Butch, you better skedaddle on back to the Sheriff, and let her know the good people of Tombstone ain't gonna stand for any more o' her guff.

MARIETTA: Yeah, we been treated like guff under her boots for too long now, and we're not gonna take it!

MAYOR: So you tell the Sheriff to wipe that guff-eatin' grin off her face and get the heck outta Dodge—

MARIETTA: *(Correcting:)* Tombstone.

MAYOR: Tombstone—or I'm gonna have to come over there myself and then the guff is really gonna hit the fan!

BUTCH: *(Calmly drawing a pistol:)* Big talk, Mayor.

MARIETTA: He's a big man.

BUTCH: He don't look so big.

MARIETTA: You haven't seen him in chaps.

BUTCH: And spurs?

MAYOR: *(Interrupting:)* Not now, Marietta. *(To* BUTCH, *backing her across the room:)* You can shoot me if you want, Butch. But if you do, you're gonna have to answer to the Count.

BUTCH: The Count?

MAYOR: Yeah, the Count. He's back in Tombstone. Rode into town last night.

BUTCH: But he's dead.

MAYOR: Oh, he's alive. Marietta saw him right here in this very saloon.

BUTCH: When?

MARIETTA: Last night, 'round about midnight, I suppose.

BUTCH: And me and my posse saw him right after that, and we shot him dead. He come to Tombstone all right. But it's a tombstone up on boot hill.

MAYOR: *(Nervous:)* You don't say?

(BUTCH *backs the* MAYOR *across the room.*)

BUTCH: So, can I still shoot you if I want?

MAYOR: *(Very nervous:)* Well, uh...I don't know, I mean... What would the Sheriff say?

BUTCH: I dunno. What do you say, Sheriff?

(*The* SHERIFF *has appeared in the doorway. Everyone gets real quiet.*)

SHERIFF: Jesse, Butch! Doc wants to see you.

BUTCH: What about this no account Mayor? Can I shoot him, Sheriff?

SHERIFF: You forgot to say the magic word, Butch.

BUTCH: *(Grins:)* Please?

(SHERIFF *turns to the* MAYOR *with a sinister gleam in her eye.*)

SHERIFF: There's worse things than killin'.

(Blackout)

(*The* MUMMY *enters with the Funeral set. On the way out, it almost runs into the wall again, but at the last second it remembers and feels for the door before exiting.*)

THE COUNT'S FUNERAL

(Several TOWNSPEOPLE *in mourning gather around the coffin. The* MAYOR, *dressed like a showgirl, delivers the eulogy.)*

MAYOR: He was a good man, a brave man, a heroic man. To his friends, he was a good friend. Friendly, and a man you could count on when the chips were down. And to his enemies? Well, let's face it, his enemies kicked his patoot and now he's dead. He was our last hope, our only hope. The one man who could have stopped the Sheriff, and now... *(At a loss for words, he gazes down into the coffin and weeps. Then he suddenly looks up from the coffin, wiping away tears.)* He's not dead!

EVERYBODY: *(Horrified:)* WHAT!!

MAYOR: As long as we remember him, he will never die!

EVERYBODY: *(Relieved and bored at the same time:)* Yeah, yeah...blah blah blah...

(They all start to leave.)

MAYOR: *(Following them out:)* No, really. We can't forget him, what he stood for... *(Etc)*

(Everyone is gone, except DELLA. *She stands over the coffin, dressed in black. A strange moaning, comes from the coffin. It grows louder, turns into a yawn. The* COUNT *sits up in his coffin, stretches.)*

COUNT: How long was I out?

DELLA: All day.

COUNT: *(Checking his wounds:)* That hurt. Well, let's get back to work. *(He climbs out of the coffin, and leaves.)*

(Blackout)

(The MUMMY *sprints on and exits with the Funeral set.)*

THE SALOON

(The SHERIFF *and a couple of her hench-deputies are playing cards.)*

DEALER: Pair o' Jacks.

JANGO: What d'ya got, Sheriff?

SHERIFF: Full house. Aces and eights.

JANGO: The dead man's hand!

SHERIFF: What?

JANGO: Aces and eights, that's the dead man's hand.

DEALER: That's right, Sheriff, that's the dead man's hand.

JANGO: You're gonna die now.

SHERIFF: I am not!

DEALER: I'm pretty sure you are—

SHERIFF: *(Drawing her gun:)* Shut up! Deal the cards and I don't want to hear no more about no dead man's hand. You got that?

CARD PLAYERS: Yeah, Sheriff. No problem, Sheriff.

SHERIFF: Good. Anybody ever tell you, you're a superstitious lot?

(They are all very quiet as the cards are dealt. The SHERIFF *looks at her cards, then suddenly throws them down and draws her gun again, grabbing the Dealer by the throat.)*

SHERIFF: Yer stackin' the deck!

DEALER: No, Sheriff, honest, I ain't stackin' the deck.

SHERIFF: Then how come I got aces and eights again?

ACT ONE

(Lightning. Suddenly the lights go out.)

SOMEONE: The lights!

(The lights start to come back on.)

JANGO: There, they're coming back.

SHERIFF: Darned kerosene lamps.

(During the blackout, the COUNT *has appeared onstage.)*

COUNT: I'm looking for the Sheriff!

(Everyone spins around startled, seeing him for the first time.)

EVERYONE: What the—?

SHERIFF: *(Very tough:)* I'm the Sheriff.

(Beat)

COUNT: No, seriously, I'm looking for the Sheriff.

SHERIFF: I'm the Sheriff!

COUNT: *(Perplexed:)* That can't be right.

SHERIFF: Why not?

COUNT: I was told that the Sheriff was a lowdown, ruthless snake-in-the-grass.

SHERIFF: That's me.

COUNT: She strikes fear in the hearts of the townspeople. That can't be you.

SHERIFF: Why can't it be me?

COUNT: Well, look at you. You're perfectly ordinary.

SHERIFF: *(Getting angry now:)* Why don't I show you just how ruthless and lowdown I can be. *(To the others:)* Fetch the gelding irons.

DOC: *(Appearing in a doorway:)* That won't be necessary, Sheriff.

SHERIFF: I can handle this, Doc.

DOC: No, I don't think you can, Sheriff. *(He enters and circles the* COUNT, *like a jungle cat:)* You see, it's true what they say about the Sheriff, Count. They still call you "The Count", do they not? She is a lowdown, ruthless, snake-in-the-grass. But as for striking fear in the heart of the townspeople. That's really my job. But I only do it part time because I am so very busy with my experiments, you know. So the Sheriff here runs things for me. However, I am the brains of the outfit. Pardon the expression.

SHERIFF: But Doc—

DOC: Silence!

COUNT: Doctor Frankenstein. It's been a very long time.

DOC: Not since our little run-in in Bavaria. Still on the wrong side of the law, I see?

COUNT: And you're still on the wrong side of nature, I presume?

DOC: Is there a right side, really?

COUNT: Not in this town.

DOC: Rumor has it you're a gunfighter now. Or should I say, "legend" has it? *(Looking him over:)* The one they call "The Count". I wonder... Are you as fast as they say you are?

(Tense moment. Suddenly, they both go for their guns. DOC *draws first and shoots the* COUNT. *The bullet goes through him and kills the* SHERIFF. *The* COUNT *draws his gun. Points it at* DOC.*)*

COUNT: How fast do they say I am?

DOC: They use the word "molasses".

COUNT: I should have known you were behind this, Doctor Frankenstein. But I don't understand why the

ACT ONE 23

people are in such fear of you, either. You're pretty handy with a gun, but I bet you're still no match for an angry mob with pitchforks and torches.

DOC: As usual, you underestimate me, Count. You must realize that brains always wins out over... *(Looks at the* COUNT:*)* Whatever you have.

COUNT: Not this time, Doc.

DOC: Oh, yes, this time. *(To the crowd:)* Citizens of Tombstone!

TOWNSPEOPLE: What?

DOC: Is this the gunfighter who will save you from my nefarious clutches?

TOWNSPEOPLE: *(In unison:)* YES! *(Then, severally:)* We think so. Sure. Why not?

DOC: Well, then, I challenge him to a duel.

COUNT: And I accept.

TOWNSPEOPLE: Hurrah!

DOC: If he can defeat me in a gunfight, I will leave your town forever.

COUNT: In a pine box.

TOWNSPEOPLE: Hurrah!

COUNT: I'm ready when you are, Doc.

DOC: Good. I shall be ready... Tomorrow?

COUNT: Tomorrow.

TOWNSPEOPLE: Hurrah!

DOC: Tomorrow at noon?

TOWNSPEOPLE: Hurrah!

COUNT: Um... High noon?

DOC: Yes, you're not busy, I hope?

COUNT: Uh, could we make it a little later?

DOC: Twelve-fifteen? Twelve-thirty?

COUNT: No, uh, more like...

TOWNSPEOPLE: What's the matter, Count? Are you a gunfighter or ain't you? What's wrong with high noon?

DOC: They're right, you know. It *is* tradition. So it's settled, we'll meet tomorrow at high noon. *(For the crowd's benefit:)* Unless you're...YELLOW-BELLIED!

(Slight booing from the crowd.)

COUNT: *(Under his breath to* DOC:*)* I'll get you for this.

DOC: *(Triumphantly:)* High noon it is!

TOWNSPEOPLE: Yahoo!

DOC: *(Aside to* COUNT:*)* You see, my dear vampire, in a contest of brains versus... whatever you've got. Brains wins every time.

*(*DOC *exits in triumph.)*

COUNT: Not this time. *(He takes the badge off the dead* SHERIFF, *pins it on himself.)* There's a new Sheriff in town.

END OF ACT ONE

ACT TWO

OLD TIMER: The sun it was burnin'
So bright in the sky.
And a crowd gathered round
Just to see a man die.
They were hungry for blood and the hot smell of lead.
But you can't kill a man, if he's already dead.

MAIN STREET

(Lights up on DOC, *poised like a gunfighter. He strides toward us, spurs jingling, his hands hover near his six-guns, as if he's about to draw. After a beat, he looks at his watch instead.)*

DOC: Where is he? It's almost noon.

(A crowd of townspeople are discovered nearby.)

TOWNSPERSON: He'll be here, don't you worry.

OTHER TOWNSPERSON: *(Murmur)* Where's he at?

*(*DELLA *enters. She is very nervous about addressing the townspeople.)*

DELLA: Ahem, I have a message from the Count.

EVERYBODY: What is it? What's going on?

DELLA: He wants me to tell you that he's very, very, very sorry for the inconvenience. But he can't make it to the gunfight today.

TOWNSPERSON: In other words, he's a no-good, yella-bellied, lily-livered, chicken-hearted...weasel-butt!

OTHER TOWNSPEOPLE: Yeah!

DELLA: No! No, he's not a weasel-butt! He's the only man in this town who ever stood up to Doc Frankenstein and his boys. And girls. *(To* DOC*)* If you were half the man the Count is—

DOC: Then I'd be a fourth of a man. The bottom line, Della, is that he's not here. Your precious Count had the chance to stop Doc Frankenstein once and for all, and he didn't have the spine to face me.

VARIOUS TOWNSPEOPLE: Yeah! Boo! Down with the Count!

DELLA: No, it's a lie! He's got spine. Plenty of it. Why, he's got backbone comin' out his ears.

TOWNSPEOPLE: Ew!

DELLA: Not literally.

TOWNSPEOPLE: Oh.

DELLA: He wanted to be here. It's just... He just... Well, it's high noon, you see, and... Well, he didn't want to mention this before, because it's kind of embarrassing...but he has very sensitive skin and too much sun isn't good for him, so, um, so...

DOC: What Miss Della is trying to say, as delicately as she can, is that the Count is missing today, not because he's afraid of me. But because he's afraid of getting a tan!

(Crowd laughs.)

DELLA: No, no, he... It's more serious than that...

DOC: *(Jovially:)* I shouldn't toy with Miss Della like this. You see, the truth of the matter is that Miss Della and I are both tellin' you a pack of lies, and I think we could

ACT TWO

both go on tossin' buffalo chips until the cows come home and it won't get us any closer to the truth.

TOWNSPERSON: What's the truth?

DOC: The truth is—and I think Miss Della will back me up on this—that the Count is neither yellow-bellied, nor a coward. And in eight or nine hours, when the sun goes down, I imagine he'll show up here and prove it by shootin' me down like a dog in the street. And then he's gonna shoot anyone else who called him a coward just now.

TOWNSPEOPLE: Uh oh.

DOC: And there won't be nothing any of us can do about it. Because in reality, the Count is not afraid of me or you or any man living. Or woman either, for that matter. And he's missing today not because he has sensitive eyes, or a skin condition, or a dentist's appointment that's keeping him from facin' me right now. No, the Count won't meet me today or any day, because he's a creature of the night. A vampire. A blood-sucking monster straight out of hell. And the truth is, he didn't come to Tombstone to set you free! HE CAME TO SUCK YOUR BLOOD!

(The crowd murmurs.)

DOC: And there is something else you should know about your brave hero. You all know him as "The Count", but his real name is Dracula. Count Dracula.

TOWNSPERSON: My God! He's European!!

DOC: That's right. And like all Europeans, he wants only one thing from you.

TOWNSPERSON: Our women?

DOC: Don't be stupid, your women are ugly.
HE WANTS TO SUCK YOUR BLOOD!

(Various shrieks of terror.)

TOWNSPERSON: Is it true, Miss Della?

DELLA: Uh, yes and no...

TOWNSPEOPLE: Agh! It's half true! Run for your lives!

(TOWNSPEOPLE *run screaming away.*)

DELLA: Wait! We've got to stick together if we're going to fight Doc Frankenstein!

TOWNSPERSON: Fight him yourself! I'm gettin' my blood indoors before the sun goes down.

(*Soon, they're all gone.*)

DELLA: (*To* DOC:) You may have won this time, Frankenstein. But the Count won't let these people down, no matter how bad you scare 'em into thinkin' he will.

(DOC *just laughs maniacally, as* DELLA *exits. The* CLANTONS *gather around.*)

BUTCH: What do we do now, Doc?

DOC: Pillage.

BUTCH: Pillage?

DOC: Yes, pillage.

(*Pause*)

BUTCH: Is that like lootin'?

DOC: Yes, it's exactly the same thing!

BUTCH: Well, why didn't you say so?

DOC: Just do it!

BUTCH: (*To the other* CLANTONS:) You heard the man, boys! And girls! Loot!

DOC: Loot like there's no tomorrow!

(*The* CLANTONS *exchange worried glances.*)

ACT TWO

JANGO: There is gonna be a tomorrow, though, isn't there?

DOC: Yes, of course, it's a figure of speech!

JANGO: But how are we gonna stop the Count? We done killed him once, but he just keeps comin' back.

DOC: Don't you worry about the Count. There's a new Sheriff in town...

(Enter the Frankenstein MONSTER. DOC *pins a badge on the* MONSTER.*)*

DOC: Now, go on, loot!

(The CLANTONS *charge off, hootin' and hollerin'.)*

(Blackout)

(The MUMMY *enters to strike the set, but there isn't one, or somebody already struck it. The* MUMMY *gropes around for it, tries to peek through its bandages. Eventually, the lights come up for the scene, and it has to hide onstage.)*

THE SALOON

(The COUNT *enters. The* PIANO PLAYER *hides. The* BARKEEP *has a big bandage on her hand.)*

COUNT: Town seems mighty quiet tonight.

BARKEEP: What'll it be... *(Not sure what to call him:)* ...uh, Sheriff?

COUNT: Sloe comfortable screw.

(Enter DELLA.*)*

COUNT: Never mind.

*(*DELLA *crosses to the bar. She slaps him.)*

COUNT: What was that for?

DELLA: For being a no show at the showdown. A drop out at the shoot out. For leading people on, and letting 'em down.

COUNT: I was in a coffin at the time, and you know it.

DELLA: I know why you weren't there. I'm not angry about that. I'm angry because folks was countin' on you, Count, and we had to count you out. It was bad enough this town being run by Doc Frankenstein, but you had to go and get our hopes up that we still had a chance. Well, fat chance of that, because you can't help us. You may be immortal and invincible. But you're no help at all.

COUNT: I think I've helped already. The town's as quiet as a mouse.

DELLA: *Now*, it's quiet. But you weren't here two hours ago. The Doc and his minions have completely run amok. What's it matter if it's safe to go out at night when people are being robbed in the streets in broad daylight? He's onto you, Count. There's no stoppin' him now. Him and his Clantons have got the run of this town as long as the sun shines. And there's nothin' you can do about it, because they'll high tail it into their hideouts by sundown. You're gonna have a hard time fightin' something that don't come out after dark.

COUNT: They don't have to come out. I'll hunt them down. I'll find them in their lairs.

DELLA: You hunt all you want, but you'll find them in the church.

COUNT: *(Nervous:)* The church?

DELLA: Yeah, the white building with the big cross on it.

COUNT: I know what a church is! *(Looks out the window:)* The one with the big cross, huh?

ACT TWO 31

DELLA: That's where they're holed up. They know you won't go in there, even at night. You're licked, Count.

COUNT: Not yet, I'm not. Call a town meeting. The citizens have got to band together. They don't need me to win this fight. I know Doc Frankenstein and he's no match for an angry mob. If they just stick together, they'll beat him. And if they have big sticks, that'll help.

DELLA: They won't come to no meetings.

COUNT: Why not?

DELLA: They're not gonna listen to you. Doc Frankenstein told 'em about your bloodsuckin' ways.

COUNT: But they'll listen to you.

DELLA: And they won't listen to me either, because I'm the one told 'em to listen to you in the first place. And even if they did listen, they won't go near that church, because they're scared to death of the new Sheriff.

COUNT: But I'm the new Sheriff.

(DOC enters.)

DOC: I'm afraid not. Sheriff-ing is a twenty-four hour job, Count, and quite frankly, you're only half-qualified.

(Several CLANTONS come in as well. They surround the COUNT.)

COUNT: Doctor Frankenstein. You made a big mistake coming here. You should have stayed in church.

DOC: I should have stayed in school, but that hasn't slowed me down.

(The COUNT makes a move toward the DOC. The deputies draw crucifixes from their holsters. The COUNT backs off.)

COUNT: Now, fellas...and gals...take it easy.

DOC: Yeah, we wouldn't want one of those holy symbols to go off prematurely. Somebody might get religion.

COUNT: Why did you come here, Frankenstein?

DOC: As a courtesy. I thought you might like to meet the new Sheriff.

(Enter the MONSTER.*)*

DOC: He has the strength of ten men.

THE MONSTER: Grrr...

(The MONSTER *picks up the* COUNT *by the lapels.)*

DELLA: He may have the strength of ten men... But can he dance?

(She puts a nickel in the juke box. The COUNT *and the* MONSTER *dance. Everybody joins in.)*

(The MUMMY *appears out of nowhere and dances with them.)*

(After the song—or after DOC *pulls the plug on the juke box:)*

DOC: Where were we?

COUNT: You'd like me to meet the new Sheriff.

DOC: He has the strength of ten men.

COUNT: He may have the strength of ten men, but is he fast?

DOC: Sheriff, draw!

(The MONSTER *goes for its gun. It is so slow that the* COUNT *beats it to the draw. The* COUNT *shoots the* MONSTER. *The* MONSTER *shoots the* COUNT. *Neither one of them dies. Beat. They both shoot each other again. Still no one dies.)*

DOC: It seems we have a standoff.

COUNT: I don't think so. *(Points his gun at* DOC:*)* What if I just kill you?

ACT TWO

DOC: A good question. The Count raises a very good question. Let us say, hypothetically... *(Looks at* COUNT:*)* That I were dead.

(He drops dead. The MONSTER *goes berserk, wailing and smashing tables. It picks up a henchman and throws him through a window. It picks up* DELLA.*)*

COUNT: No!

DOC: *(Jumping up:)* Oh, look, I'm okay! My goodness, I gave myself quite a scare. So... Anything exciting happen while I was dead?

COUNT: All right, I see your point. *(Pointing at a random henchman:)* But what's to keep me from killing this guy?

DOC: Nothing. *(He shoots the deputy himself.)* But you see, that is exactly my point. I can loot and pillage the town all day long. And you can spend the whole night unlooting it, and tearing down everything I build up. Or vice versa. My people will live in fear of the sunset, and yours in fear of the sunrise. We can go back and forth like that forever. Neither of us can win. Neither of us can lose. But the people. The innocent bystanders like Miss Molly here. *(He shoots the Barkeep.)* Or Della...

(He points his gun at DELLA. *The* COUNT *grabs his arm, twists it a bit.)*

DOC: *(Calmly, for the* MONSTER's *benefit:)* Ow.

THE MONSTER: Rrrrrr...

(The COUNT *releases* DOC's *arm.)*

DOC: They will pay the price for our squabbling. Soon you will be Sheriff over fifteen acres of rubble. And so will I. *(Pointing at* MONSTER:*)* Or he will, rather. And who wants that?

COUNT: So what do you suggest?

DOC: I propose a compromise.

COUNT: No deal, Doc. I won't let you bully the good people of Tombstone. Even for half a day.

DOC: I wouldn't expect you to. But I am not an unreasonable man. Only evil. And I think that if we sat down and talked about it, you and I could eventually come to some sort of an agreement.

DELLA: Don't trust him, Count.

DOC: No, of course not. Please, don't trust me. It puts you in such a bad bargaining position. But we can *talk*, can't we?

COUNT: Okay. Let's talk.

DOC: Excellent! A round of drinks! To talk by. What'll you have? No, wait, allow me. *(He goes behind the bar.)* Miss Della, have you ever enjoyed a Screaming Orgasm?

DELLA: Not in this town.

DOC: Excellent. And for the Count and myself... *(He begins mixing a pair of drinks.)* Orange juice... a little grenadine...

(The COUNT *sits down at a table.* DOC *brings their drinks over.)*

DOC: *(Toasting:)* To our new partnership. And a brighter tomorrow! Or a darker.

(They drink.)

COUNT: This is tasty. What's in it?

DOC: Mostly orange juice and tequila.

COUNT: Tequila? Hmm.

DOC: It's called a Tequila Sunrise.

(The COUNT *drops his glass and leaps up, screaming in agony.)*

COUNT: Sunrise!!

ACT TWO

(DOC throws his own Tequila Sunrise in the COUNT's face as well. The COUNT screams and writhes in pain.)

DOC: Now!

(The CLANTONS pull out their crucifixes and surround the Count. DOC pounces on him with a mallet and a wooden stake. The MONSTER holds DELLA, while DOC drives the stake through the COUNT's heart.)

(Blackout)

(The MUMMY gropingly makes it's way offstage to fetch the next set. While it is still fumbling for the doorway, the Funeral set zips in, apparently hurled onstage by an impatient stagehand. The MUMMY shrugs, exits.)

THE COUNT'S FUNERAL

MAYOR: *(Eulogizing:)* He was a good man, a brave man, and a horrible demonic creature straight out of hell and thank God we're rid of him. Now maybe this town can get back to normal. ...But somehow I doubt it.

(Everybody leaves, except DELLA. She stands over the coffin.)

DELLA: *(Bitter, tearful:)* I want you to know that this is the last time I'm coming to one of your funerals.

(No response.)

DELLA: All right, I'll tell you what. If you come back to life, I'll come to one more funeral, but then that's it.

(Still no response. In sudden desperation, DELLA hurls herself upon the corpse and tugs at the wooden stake, but it doesn't come out.)

DELLA: *(Breaking down:)* Please, please, don't be dead, you no good son of a gun! Please!! *(She continues to weep.)*

(Blackout)

(The MUMMY *comes in to get the Funeral set. As it is leaving, it recognizes someone in the audience. It peeks through the bandages, waves at its friend and then goes off.*)

THE SALOON

(*Crowded saloon, cheerful piano music, guns going off. The* BARKEEP *has a bandaged hand and a bandaged head.* DOC *is counting his money.*)

DOC: Quiet, I'm trying to count!

(*Everyone hoots and hollers more quietly.* JOSIE *enters.*)

JOSIE: Here's the loot from the stagecoach. What do you want me to do with it?

DOC: Take the money, and donate it to charity.

JOSIE: Charity? Really?

DOC: No, I'm joking. Go buy me a horse.

JOSIE: Yes, sir.

DOC: No, on second thought. Leave the money here and go steal me a horse.

JOSIE: Yes, sir!

JESSE: *(Entering:)* We drove the Indians off their reservation and we rustled all the cattle. What's next?

DOC: It's almost ten o'clock. The bank should be open.

JESSE: Rob it?

DOC: Please.

(JESSE *goes out, as* JOSIE *rushes back in.*)

DOC: That was fast. What'd you get?

JOSIE: He's back!

DOC: Who's back?

ACT TWO 37

JOSIE: The Count, I saw him. I barely escaped with my life.

DOC: If you saw the Count, then you barely escaped with your wits. Now go back and get me my horse.

JOSIE: No, please, don't make me go out there.

(JOSIE *cowers at* DOC'S *feet.*)

DOC: You're pathetic. All in favor of shooting this one?

(JESSE *rushes in.*)

JESSE: Doc!

DOC: What happened at the bank?

JESSE: He's back!

DOC: Who's back?

JESSE: The Count.

DOC: He is not.

JESSE: I saw him.

DOC: You did not. Let go of my feet.

JANGO: *(Rushing in:)* He's back!

DOC: Who's back?

JANGO: The Count.

DOC: All right, stop. The Count is not back, he's dead, I killed him myself. And you all helped.

JESSE: We killed him before and he came back.

DOC: Before, you didn't use a wooden stake. Trust me, this time the vampire is dead.

JANGO: But we saw him!

DOC: You did not. Obviously you are all suffering from some sort of mass delusion. Now, I'm going to get to the bottom of this. *(Takes out a pad of paper:)* Tell me about your childhood.

(They all start telling him about their childhood.)

DOC: Never mind, bad idea. We'll do this some other way.

BUTCH: *(Rushing in:)* He's back!

DOC: He is not. Now sit down here and cower with the rest of them. Even if he were not dead, which he is, the vampire would not be wandering about in broad daylight, as you claim.

MONSTER: *(Rushing in:)* Uuhn! *(He's back!)*

DOC: Not you, too. *(To the others:)* Now, look what you've done.

JANGO: *(Panicking:)* We gotta get out of here, boss. What if he finds us? He's unbeatable! Unkillable!! Unstoppable!!!

(DOC shoots JANGO.)

DOC: Okay, I'm making a new rule. No one can speak when they're hysterical.

(A caped figure appears in the doorway.)

DELLA: (Caped figure) Can they scream?

(Lightning. The lights go out. Screams and gunfire. When the lights come back on, most of the DOC's minions have fled or shot each other. DOC backs away from the caped figure in fear.)

DOC: Who are you? What are you? You're dead! I know you are! *(Suddenly figuring it out:)* Wait a minute...

(He grabs the figure and spins it around. It's Batman!)

CLANTONS: It's Batman!

(DOC pulls off the Batman mask. It's DELLA!)

ACT TWO 39

CLANTONS: It's Della!

DOC: Well, you've given us quite a little scare, Miss Della. I should congratulate you, but I'm in such a foul mood. *(To the fallen henchmen:)* Jesse! Josie!

(Nobody moves. They're all dead. DOC *sighs, exasperated.)*

DOC: Butch!

*(*BUTCH *jumps up.)*

BUTCH: Yes sir?

DOC: Take her out to the town square.

DELLA: What are you going to do to me?

DOC: I'm going to surgically reconstruct your internal organs with electrodes and mechanical parts. And extract your brain and vivisect it into a dozen bite-sized morsels and rearrange them in no particular order and put some of them back and replace the rest with wires and circuitry, and weld it all together into something vaguely resembling the woman you once were, only better, more fuel efficient. ...But first I have to kill you. Take her away!

*(*BUTCH *exits with* DELLA.*)*

THE MONSTER: Hrrm...?

DOC: What are you looking at? She's not for you. This one is mine! All mine! *(Dreamy:)* I will program her to love me like no other, and I will dress her up in that frilly red frock I've always admired, and I will take her to the hoe down. And we will dance and dance and dance... *(Sinister:)* And everybody will have a good time...

(Blackout)

(The MUMMY *enters with the Hanging set. It is a little complicated to set up, and the* MUMMY *ends up staying*

onstage for most of the next scene. It gets the set finished just in time for the hanging.)

THE TOWN SQUARE

(Near the hanging tree. BUTCH *and* JETHRO *are preparing to hang* DELLA.*)*

BUTCH: Miss Della, do you understand the charges against you?

DELLA: *(Gagged:)* Mmph!

JETHRO: Hey, she sounds like the new Sheriff.

(They laugh. Then they become self-conscious.)

JETHRO: You won't tell him we said that, will ya?

DELLA: Mmph!

BUTCH: Thank you, ma'am, we appreciate it.

(They continue stringin' her up. Doc enters, speaks to a crowd that has gathered round.)

DOC: People of Tombstone, here ends the legend of the Count. Here ends the myth. Let the inscription on his tomb read: "He was a brave man. But he died like a woman." Hang her.

JETHRO: Any last words, Miss Della?

DELLA: Mmph, mmph, mmph!

JETHRO: Amen to that.

*(*BUTCH *takes the gag off.)*

DELLA: He's not dead! The Count will never die. As long as there is a spark of resistance in anyone's heart, it will ignite the flame of defiance, and the Count will live. He is in each of us, and he is in all of us. We are all Count Dracula! I am Count Dracula!

ACT TWO

SOMEONE: *(Stepping out of the crowd:)* I am Count Dracula!

SOMEONE ELSE: *(Stepping out of the crowd:)* I am Count—

(The CLANTONS *draw their guns and cock them.)*

SOMEONE ELSE: I take it back, I'm not Count Dracula.

SOMEONE: Me neither.

DOC: Good. Now if there are no more theatrics—

CAPED FIGURE: *(Stepping out of the crowd:)* I am Count Dracula!

DOC: *(Perturbed:)* Okay, new rule: no one can speak when I'm irritated.

CAPED FIGURE: Can they scream?

(The caped figure turns around. It's the COUNT*! Almost everyone screams and runs about. The* COUNT *fights with three or four of* DOC's *lackeys. He wins, of course. Finally, it's just* DOC *and the* COUNT.*)*

DOC: You wouldn't hurt an unarmed man.

COUNT: What makes you say that?

DOC: *(Shrugs:)* It was worth a try.

*(*DOC *goes for his gun. The* COUNT *goes for his gun, too.* DOC *draws first and he shoots...*DELLA*!)*

COUNT: Noooo!

DELLA: Ouch.

*(*DELLA *collapses. The* COUNT *rushes to her side.* DOC *makes his getaway.)*

DELLA: I knew you'd come back.

COUNT: I never should have left.

DELLA: I never should have let you go. *(She is dying.)* Kiss me.

(He kisses her. Then, he bites her neck.)

(Blackout)

(The MUMMY *comes in to dismantle the Hanging set. Once again, it has a hard time with it, ends up tangled up in the rope, staggers about the stage, crashing into things and becoming more and more entangled in the pieces of the Hanging set. Eventually it collapses in a heap near the door. A hand reaches in from offstage, and drags the* MUMMY *off.)*

THE SALOON

*(*DOC *has gathered the remaining* CLANTONS *and the* MONSTER *in the saloon to arm themselves for one last stand. He hands them a box of produce.)*

BUTCH: *(Looking in the box:)* What's this for?

DOC: Garlic. Everybody take some.

(They all take a clove.)

DOC: Stakes?

(They all hold up their stakes.)

DOC: Crucifix? Mirror?

(They all show this equipment as well.)

DOC: All right, I do not know what went wrong last time, but this time the vampire's going down for the count. We'll hide out here till morning, then at daybreak, we'll find him, pound stakes into his heart, decapitate him and immerse his headless corpse in a vat of holy water. Any questions?

COUNT: *(Appearing in the doorway:)* What if he shows up before morning?

(The bad guys quickly brandish their crucifixes. The COUNT *recoils, melodramatically.)*

ACT TWO   43

COUNT: HSSS!! *(But then:)* Oh my. Sorry about that, must be my allergies acting up. I'm fine now.

DOC: Mirrors!

(They brandish their mirrors.)

COUNT: For me? How sweet. These will go with my handbag.

BUTCH: *(To* DOC:*)* Shall we try the garlic?

COUNT: Not unless you're going to sauté me.

(The COUNT *tosses a couple* CLANTONS *aside and grabs the* DOC.*)*

DOC: I put a stake through your heart, damn you!

COUNT: I know, and it hurt like the dickens.

DOC: *(Flailing at him:)* What does it take to kill you?

COUNT: Have you tried silver bullets?

DOC: On a vampire?

COUNT: Did I say I was a vampire? I'm sorry, I thought you knew... I'm a werewolf.

(The COUNT *turns and we see that he is, indeed, a werewolf.)*

DOC: Noooooo!

COUNT: Yep.

(The COUNT *strangles* DOC. *The* MONSTER *goes berserk and attacks the* COUNT, *momentarily freeing* DOC. *While* DOC *tries to catch his breath, the* COUNT *and the* MONSTER *fight. They are pretty evenly matched.)*

(Suddenly DELLA *comes in, puts a nickel in the juke box. Music plays. The* MONSTER *stops fighting and starts to dance. The* COUNT *leaps onto its back and unplugs the* MONSTER's *extension cord. The* MONSTER *grinds to a halt. The* COUNT *climbs off its back, panting for breath.)*

COUNT: Whew.

(DOC *leaps up, grabs* DELLA *and holds a gun to her head.*)

DOC: All right, Count, I'm through playing games. One false move and Della gets a bullet in her pretty little head.

DELLA: I hope those are silver bullets.

DOC: Why? Oh no.

DELLA: Grrr...

(DOC *lets her go and runs out of the room.* DELLA *bounds after him.* DOC *is hurled back into the room, landing behind the bar.* DELLA *reenters, she is a werewolf.* DELLA *and the* COUNT *both leap over the bar and pounce on* DOC. *Body parts fly everywhere. When they finally come up for air, they are no longer werewolves.*)

COUNT: I guess Doc Frankenstein was wrong when he said that brains always wins out over brawn.

DELLA: Now, Count, what he actually said was that brains wins out over "whatever you've got".

COUNT: And what we've got is character, courage.

DELLA: And a just cause.

COUNT: And our hearts in the right place.

DELLA: And good friends at our sides.

COUNT: And when you've got all that. What's a little brain?

DELLA: (*Holding* DOC's *brain:*) Not much, I guess.

(*She tosses it aside.* DELLA *and the* COUNT *kiss. Happy ending music swells.*)

DELLA: (*As they go off together:*) And fangs. We got fangs.

COUNT: Fangs are good.

DELLA: Brains versus fangs.

COUNT: No contest.

ACT TWO

DELLA: And we're bulletproof.

(They go out the door and off into the sunset.)

OLD TIMER: And they disappeared into
That crimson sunset.
But the legend lives on,
And I'll never forget
That I heard them exclaim as they rode out of sight,
"Happy Halloween all. Hope we gave you a fright."

(Howling off in the distance, as the sun goes down.)

(Blackout)

END OF PLAY

CPSIA information can be obtained
at www.ICGtesting.com
Printed in the USA
LVHW011947201220
674716LV00006B/128